# Fire Your Pastor:

## Rediscovering New Testament Church

By Lonnie Wibberding

This book was originally published in 2009 by Big Fish
Publishing under the title: "Fire Your Pastor: The Hope of
a Lost World." It has been reprinted in 2017 by
101.church with minor changes.

If you would like an electronic version of this book you
can get one on the web at:

**101.church/fireyourpastor**

# Acknowledgements

Seldom is any accomplishment the work of one man. This book is no exception. I'd like to especially thank the following individuals that contributed to my development and therefore to this project. Some gave me an example of self-sacrificing mission. Others created an environment where I could minister. Still others challenged my thinking. Thanks to:

Jim Kincaid

Milton Adams

Russell Burrill

# Table of Contents

# Introduction

I hope you enjoy this book. But you may not. Once you finish reading you may feel like the guy who was a faithful churchgoer. He paid his tithe. He supported the church with his time. He did everything he knew was right. Then one day he discovered he was going to church on a day God never set aside as holy.

As you can imagine this was quite a shock. He had meant well for decades but was doing the wrong thing.

My prayer is that it helps you better fulfill the calling God has given you.

# Chapter 1

## How to Become Poor Eating Doughnuts

The value of what we do is more important than it seems. I was looking over my retirement plan the other day and it struck me: Every dollar I can save is worth more to me than a dollar I spend because of compounding interest. This becomes clear with a simple example.

Imagine I love doughnuts. Unfortunatly, this won't require a lot of imagination. But let's say I really love doughnuts. In fact, I love doughnuts so much I buy one every day, five days a week. Each doughnut cost me fifty cents. Each week I spend two dollars and fifty cents. Each month ten dollars.

But one day I get the victory. Doughnuts are a thing of the past. I put my two quarters aside and instead put them in a mutual fund that earns a nice twelve percent per year.

In ten years I have $2,323. In twenty I have $9,991, and in thirty $35,299, even though I only put in $3,600 over a period of thirty years. For each fifty cent doughnut I bought, I gave up $4.90 thirty years later. Expensive doughnuts.

The idea of compounding interest is a very powerful one. This idea that money can earn interest, then earn interest on the interest and so on has made more than one man wealthy.

This may be good financial advice, but my purpose is not to make you rich. There are other books on that. However, thinking along these lines allows us to see problems and solutions we may miss otherwise.

Let's take a look, not at compounding money, but compound growth. The same principle that has built many a person's kingdom, has also helped build God's kingdom.

## *Church growth percentages*

In 1863 the Seventh-day Adventist church was organized. There was a big debate on whether organization was biblical, or whether it was the way of the world. Finally, the early Adventist's came to a decision. To efficiently fulfill mission, organization was necessary. And praise God that they did! The church began to grow.

Early statistics are hard to come by. We can estimate the church membership was about 3,500 when the general conference was formed in 1863[1].

During those first 37 years the church saw some wonderful growth (some years growing by around 20%). Overall, between the years 1863 and 1900 the church grew on average 8.9% per year. That's good consistent growth.

Remember compounding interest? It works with church growth too. The church was exploding! By 1900 instead of 3,500, we find church membership up to 75,767[2], over twenty-one times its original size. What is interesting though is it only had to grow 8.9% per year to get there.

I wonder what the church leaders were thinking around 1900? Some may have thought, "Okay, we have growth on average 8.9% each year for the last 37 years. How long will it take to reach the world?"

Their calculations may have looked something like this.

## *Projected growth to 1 billion members*

Year                  Projected at 8.9% growth per year

---

[1] 1863- 1900 report found at www.AdventistStatistics.org

[2] www.AdventistStatistics.org

| | |
|---|---|
| 1900 | 75,676 |
| 1910 | 178,003 |
| 1920 | 418,191 |
| 1930 | 982,476 |
| 1940 | 2,308,178 |
| 1950 | 5,422,716 |
| 1960 | 12,739,852 |
| 1970 | 29,930,359 |
| 1980 | 70,316,858 |
| 1990 | 165,198,840 |
| 2000 | 388,109,729 |
| *2008* | *768,621,552* |
| 2010 | 911,805,200 |
| 2012 | 1,081,661,998 |

It would have been reasonable knowing annual growth rates for 37 years in 1900 to predict reaching 1 billion people with the Gospel by 2012. That would be reasonable. However, if you are familiar with membership numbers in the Adventist Church you know we have around 16 million members in 2008, not 768 million.

What happened? Unfortunately, the growth rate of 8.9% per year didn't keep up. Here are actual growth rates for each decade since 1900.

# Actual membership growth since 1900

| Year | Percentage | Membership[3] |
|------|-----------|---------------|
| 1900-10 | 3.2% | 100,931 |
| 1910-20 | 5.8% | 178,239 |
| 1920-30 | 5.3% | 299,555 |
| 1930-40 | 5.0% | 486,670 |
| 1940-50 | 3.9% | 716,538 |
| 1950-60 | 5.2% | 1,194,070 |
| 1960-70 | 5.0% | 1,953,078 |
| 1970-80 | 5.4% | 3,308,191 |
| 1980-90 | 6.6% | 6,260,617 |
| 1990-2000 | 5.7% | 10,939,182 |
| 2001 | 6.8% | 11,687,239 |
| 2002 | 5.4% | 12,320,844 |
| 2003 | 4.7% | 12,894,015 |
| 2004 | 4.0% | 13,406,554 |
| 2005 | 4.0% | 13,936,932 |

Never again in any decade do we find a worldwide growth rate of over 6.6%, let alone an average of 8.9%

---

[3] Membership at end of decade

7

## North America growth rate

Growth rates in North America are particularly interesting. The Adventist church started keeping separate statistics for North America in 1913. Here are the average annual growth rates since then, with actual growth rates the last few years in the North American Division.

| Years | Percentage | Membership |
|---|---|---|
| 1913-20 | 4.9% | 95,645 |
| 1920-30 | 2.1% | 117,771 |
| 1930-40 | 4.2% | 177,341 |
| 1940-50 | 3.2% | 243,193 |
| 1950-60 | 3.0% | 325,882 |
| 1960-70 | 2.7% | 426,295 |
| 1970-80 | 3.2% | 585,050 |
| 1980-90 | 2.4% | 743,023 |
| 1990-2000 | 2.1% | 914,106 |
| 2001 | 2.2% | 933,935 |
| 2002 | 2.3% | 955,076 |
| 2003 | 2.0% | 974,271 |
| 2004 | 1.8% | 992,046 |
| 2005 | 1.4% | 1,006,317 |

4.9% is the best rate of growth in North America since separate statistics were kept and that was the first few years.

## What happened to 98% of our people?

A provocative question arises. Why do we only have about 16 million members in 2008 when we projected to have over 768 million? We only have 2 percent of what we were projected to have.

Just like the money spent on doughnuts compounds and 50 cents becomes $4.90, membership growth also compounds. More members means more workers to reach more people. There is a huge difference between 16 million and 768 million. We should be 48 times as big as we are. We are missing 752 million people!

Did something happen in the world that was beyond our control? Did society change so we are not able to be as effective? Some would argue society did change and that is why we are not able to be so effective. It's an easy answer because the blame can be placed on someone else. But this ignores the fact that society also changed between 1863 and 1900. Different cultures developed, yet we continued our growth. However, if we are open to self-evaluation we will discover a more likely answer.

As the Adventist church moved into the 1900's, a slow drift occurred in how we conducted ministry. As you will soon discover, this change may have cost us 98% of our church membership.

# Chapter 2

## Protecting Small Gains and Missing Larger Ones, or the Parable of the Talents.

Before we go to the missing 98 percent, let's start at the beginning and answer some basic questions. Questions like: Why does the church exist? Why did Jesus create it, and how did He intend to keep it focused?

### *Jesus method to change the world*

If you were Jesus, how would you get the Good News of salvation to the world? I know, angels. I always wondered why He uses people. But if you only have people, how would you do it?

As a student of prophecy Jesus knew he had three and a half years to accomplish His mission of dying for the sins of the world and establishing His church to spread the Good News of salvation. He is baptized at age thirty, the

11

Holy Spirit descends on Him and it's time to start ministry.

What would you do? My mind starts to figure out a strategic plan. *Okay, let's see, we will need to raise money for a media campaign. And we will need as many people as we can find to get the word out. Send runners. Contact the powers that be and work through the established structure.*

But Jesus doesn't have any money. He could have. He could have had Himself born into a rich family. One who could finance a media campaign to change the thinking of the world.

Jesus doesn't use the existing power structures either. They were against Him. Even if they were on His side the message would have been contaminated because their agenda was not His agenda.

What crazy odds of success. Even with money and influence it's a dicey proposition to take the Good News to the world. Jesus starts with nothing except the Holy Spirit He receive at His baptism.

Mark 3:13-15 tells us what He chose to do:

*Jesus went up on a mountainside and called to him those he wanted, and they came to him. He appointed twelve—designating them apostles— that they might be with him and that he might send them out to preach and to have authority to drive out demons.*

As we think about this record of Jesus choice of ministry structure, questions come to mind. Why did Jesus choose twelve to be with Him? Why not twenty? Why not a hundred? Why even choose any to be with Him? Why not just teach the crowds?

I would suggest Jesus knew, to turn the world right side up, He would need to train some more thoroughly than the crowds. Jesus taught the crowds, but He chose twelve to train them more closely – to be with Him. They would be the ones who would start His church.

John Maxwell, a Christian minister who has studied leadership for over thirty years, suggests that everything rises and falls on leadership[4]. The success of any endeavor requires leadership. If there is good leadership the endeavor will most likely succeed. If there is bad or no leadership it is doomed to fail. It's an audacious claim Maxwell makes, but it's also true.

When we think of any group of people that want to accomplish something, leadership is necessary to get it

---

[4] Maxwell, John. *21 Indispensable Qualities of a Leader, p. XI*

13

done. It may not be a leader who is appointed as leader, but someone has to say, "Here is where we need to go and this is how we can get there." Without someone taking this initiative a group of people will go nowhere.

We see this trend throughout the Old Testament. Without people like Daniel, Gideon, David, Esther, Elijah, Ruth, and so many others God chose to work through, nothing would be done.

So we find Jesus, who has taken on the form and weakness of a man, relies on His heavenly Father's wisdom, and after a night of prayer to His Father chooses twelve.

In the hands of these twelve would rest the future of His church. The church whose very purpose is to spread the Good News that there is a Way out of this doomed planet. If they fail, the church will fail and ultimately Jesus mission will fail because nobody will know.

What a crazy risk to take! So many times it looks like Jesus has made the wrong choice. Fighting among themselves, disagreements about who will be the greatest plague the group. They misunderstand the Gospel and offer to call fire down from heaven on those who reject Jesus. They're appalled at the idea Jesus would talk to the Samaritan woman.

After three and a half years Jesus leaves them. It seems they are no better off then when He was with them. It seems Jesus plan to spread the Good News through His church has already failed. Then Pentecost comes . . .

Something happens. Those three and a half years with Jesus start to pay off. Now they are men who have been trained, but they are also men who have been baptized by the Holy Spirit. These two key components create a church that explodes in growth.

Jesus knows what He's doing after all (we kind of expected it, didn't we?). The training He gives these men is not wasted. But it takes some time to pay off. And it takes the power of the Holy Spirit.

Was this formula just for Jesus to use? Is it just Jesus who should train leaders and depend on the Spirit?

## Paul's method of changing the world

We see this idea of the importance of leadership again in the New Testament. Paul is writing to a young "pastor". He has left him behind on a missionary journey. He writes to give him instruction. In His wisdom the Holy Spirit sees fit to give us the record to learn from.

*The reason I left you in Crete was that you might straighten out what was left unfinished and appoint elders in every town, as I directed you.* Titus 1:5

Titus's job is to *set in order what remains* and *appoint elders in every town.* It sounds like a simple mission until we look at the scope of the job.

Crete is an island in the Mediterranean that spans 165 miles east to west and ten to twenty miles wide north to south for a total land mass of 3,219 square miles[5]. That's a huge landmass for one man (and he didn't have a car). But Paul understands the way Jesus ministered. Jesus spent major time with twelve, which would then teach others and they teach others. So Paul tells Titus, your job is to appoint elders and set up what remains. Set up the leadership and the structure of ministry.

Titus is left as the only paid clergy on the island. Today we would use the name *Pastor* to describe Titus' position. He has over 3,000 square miles of territory to cover, and Paul says, "You're in charge." What would you do in this situation?

You or I may, because of the culture we find ourselves in, go to the biggest church on the island and start being a

[5] Wikipedia "Crete"

pastor. When the church grows enough to support another pastor, hire a pastor for the neighboring church. Continue to do this until every church on the island of Crete has a paid pastor.

But this is not what Paul instructs Titus to do. He says, "Straighten out what is left unfinished and appoint elders in every town." Under the wisdom of the Holy Spirit, Paul gives a plan. Titus must set up a working structure and *appoint* elders in each town. Notice he does not say *elect* elders in every town. In fact nowhere in the New Testament are elders elected, they are always appointed. Deacons are elected, but never elders. We will get to the reason for this later.

This is a different model than what we usually see in the Adventist Church in North America. Usually we put a paid pastor over a church to lead it. But Paul instructs Titus to leave the local work in the hands of elders that he appoints.

Why does Paul tell Titus to appoint elders? Isn't it risky to leave the church in the hands of local elders? What if they teach erroneous doctrine and the church starts to become congregational in structure? What if the elder doesn't do his or her job and the church has weak leadership? As we mentioned before, everything rises and falls on leadership.

Since the New Testament model of ministry is so foreign to the structure in North America today, let's take a minute to think about the risks Paul and Titus were taking. Risks we try to protect ourselves from today.

## The risks of giving people leadership

The New Testament model is a risky model. It's risky because a lot depends on the local leader. If the elders who are left in charge in a town don't do their job, the church they are leading may flounder and lose focus. Remember what we said about leadership: Every group must have a leader to accomplish their mission. If there is no one to lead, nothing will get done.

The other threat comes from leaders who have strange ideas. What if one of the local elders gets ideas that are not in the Bible and leads the church off into heresy? You could lose half a church just by leaving a church under a local elder instead of a paid pastor who has been sent to seminary to understand the Bible. The idea of leaving a church under a local elder makes many people nervous because of these risks. But let's consider the other option Titus had.

## *The risks of not giving people leadership*

He could have installed himself as the pastor of one of the churches in Crete. The church may have flourished. Titus might have had great pastoral skills, but the other churches in Crete would have faltered and the kingdom's growth would depend on tithe to support it. Growth may still happen, but not at the same rate the model Paul suggests. And remember, rates matter! If we had kept our 8.9% growth rate we had before 1900 we would have 768 million instead of 16 million members today. It seems like a small issue but makes a big difference.

Instead of recommending a paid pastor for every church, Paul tells Titus to concentrate on two things. Set things in order and appoint elders. This task was so important he even gives Titus a list of what to look for in an elder. And why not, these people would be the pastors of the churches!

In the modern church, by trying to protect our theology we have sacrificed growth. I'm all for protecting truth. If we don't have the truth about Jesus there is no reason for growth. But Paul is not concerned about putting a paid pastor over every church to protect truth. As we will discover, the New Testament church uses other methods to protect truth – methods that don't slow the growth of the church.

## *The apostles keep moving*

The second growth principle we find among the apostles is how they used the rest of their time. Setting up leadership in local churches didn't take all their time. The rest was spent planting churches. We especially see this in Paul's ministry as he travels from place to place, raising up churches, putting the leadership into the hands of good men and women, and moving on.

It's a very different model then we see today, yet the church grew fast. Which brings up the pressing question, "Could we use it again and grow faster than we are today?"

It's foreign enough to make some doubt whether we could do it. A church without a paid pastor seems unrealistic. Would it be possible for all the paid clergy to become church planters or evangelists? It's a bold ministry model that is found in the New Testament, and as we will discover, in the early Adventist 8.9% growth rate church.

## *Visioning: What could be*

Could we do it again? What would happen if we used the paid pastors in North America to setup leadership in the local churches, and use the rest of their time to plant new churches?

If we took seriously the example the Holy Spirit has left for us in Titus 1:5 about leadership structure, and used the paid clergy as church planters, could we really increase our growth rate above 1.74% in North America?

As a person who loves the truth Jesus has revealed, and has a desire to share this Good News with your country, I invite you to vision with me for a few paragraphs. Let's think for a few minutes what could happen if we again followed the New Testament model.

Here is where we are today.[6]

North American Adventist information as of 2006

| | |
|---|---|
| Churches | 5,167 |
| Companies | 677 |
| Membership | 1,041,685 |
| Pastors[7] | 3,498 |
| Population | 334,530,088 |
| Land Mass | 5,322,431 miles$^2$ |

From the data above we can do some simple calculations and arrive at the figures below:

| | |
|---|---|
| Churches per pastor | 1.48 |
| Population per pastor | 95,635 |
| Population per member | 321 |
| Land mass per pastor | 1,522 miles$^2$ |
| Land mass per member | 5.11 miles$^2$ |

---

[6] Taken from 2006 Annual Report (p. 20,46) found at www.AdventistStatistics.org and https://www.cia.gov/library/publications/the-world-factbook/geos/us.html#Intro. Population and landmass are a combination of United States and Canada figures.

[7] Based on Ministerial credentials.

22

What would happen if we went back to a biblical structure of ministry? Set aside the concerns about leaving churches in the hands of elders. Also set aside the questions on how we would get there from here. Both these issue will be dealt with later. Let's just think for a minute what could happen. Consider three "What ifs."

## What if each conference in North America created districts based on geographical lines?

Every square inch of land within the conference is assigned to some paid pastor as part of a district. This does two things. First, it assigns someone to be responsible to outreach to every town, every street, every block, every house in a conference. Rarely is this done since pastors spend most of their time working with the members of the church and don't have time to think about the outside world. Second, it changes the dynamics of church. When the pastor is held accountable by the conference for the territory, he or she has to think differently and become, not just a leader, but a trainer of leaders. Too often pastors are praised when the church grows, not when their territory is reached for Jesus.

## What if a pastor spent one year training elders to run the church?

In one year the elders know they will be responsible for running their churches. The pastor will still be around for advice and occasional training, but the majority of his or her time will be spent planting churches.

## What if the pastor spent 9/10ths of her time planting a church somewhere in the district?

She spends 36 hours a week (assuming a 40 hour week) working on planting a church and 4 hours a week training leaders at the established churches.

If we chose to carry out these three steps what will happen? We can't know for sure until we try it, but here is a plausible scenario.

3,498 pastors train elders for one year. After this year is over the pastors set out somewhere inside their territory to plant a new church. It takes awhile to build relationships in the community, but after three years of working 36 hours a week trying to plant a church, the efforts pay off and there is a new church of 20 members.

Unrealistic? It's been done before even by pastors who don't spend $9/10^{th}$ of their time building relationships in the community. But let's just say for sake of argument that sadly not every one of those new church plants succeed. Some fail, wasting time and money in the process. In fact, let's assume half of all the church planting pastors in North America fail. A full fifty percent! The church pays 1,749 pastors to work a combined total of over 3 million hours for three years and they fail.

Because of the terrible waste of half our resources we only have 1,749 new churches. Add these to the 5,844 existing companies and churches gives us 7,593 churches and companies. As we waste half our resources we have 30% more churches.

Of course this is not 30% membership growth. But we've planted a church that will never need a pastor and can grow and birth new churches. And it's healthy because the members are not relying on a pastor to minister to them.

Isn't that better than paying for over 6 million hours in the same time period on those who already know Jesus and planting no new churches?

The point is, with the limited resources we have, we cannot afford to do things the way we've been doing them. 1.74% growth is not success. We need to do things the New Testament way. Only when we turn leadership over to Spirit filled men and women and let the pastors train and plant churches will the work be finished. We have spent a lot of time and money slowing the church down. It's time to stop.

As a pastor it feels good to have people look to me. It makes me feel important, and the years of school I went through to be a pastor seems worthwhile. But I would suggest my ego has been stroked at the cost of the eternal life of some. That cost is too high. The total cost may be three-quarters of a billion people who could have been part of this movement but are missing. It's true God may have found another way to save them. He is that kind of God. But it is sobering evidence that demands some answers.

How did a church that grew an average of 8.9% in 37 years slow to a North American growth rate of only 1.74% last year?[8] That's the topic of the next chapter.

---

[8] 2006

# Chapter 3

# How We Missed the Boat, or the 98% Question

If you have read the book, *Revolution in the Church*, by Russell Burrill you will find this story familiar. It is the story of good people dedicated to mission. People who had a message and had a reason to live – to tell the world about a Savior who loves them enough to come first to die, and come a second time to take them home. It's a great message that is truly Good New[9]. With fire in their hearts and urgency in their steps the early Adventists' first goal in life was to take this message, this good news to the world.

## *Organization for mission*

In 1863 after some debate over the advantages of organization the General Conference was formed. Some believed organization was part of Babylon and wanted

---

[9] The Greek word for "gospel" literally means "good news."

nothing to do with it. However, many understood the fledgling church would be stronger, and could accomplish more through a structure.

They were right. In 1863 the church had an estimated 3,500 members. By the turn of the century it had grown to 75,767. This new structure created a healthy church. Though there were inevitable bumps along the way, the church was growing and the everlasting gospel was going throughout the world.

These were grand times. God was alive. He was moving and the people of God were effective in their missionary outreach. In fact this was so noticeable a newspaper of the time decided to run an article on why Adventists were growing so rapidly. It appeared in the October 1, 1886 *Plain Dealer* in Wabash, Indiana.[10]

THE SEVENTH DAY ADVENTISTS

Some Facts and Figures Gathered from Elder Starr – How they have Grown in Forty Years – and What They Believe.

*"By what means have you carried forward your work so rapidly?"*

---

[10] Burrill, Russell, *Revolution in the Church p. 39,40*

*"Well, in the first place," replied the Elder, "we have no settled pastors. Our churches are taught largely to take care of themselves, while nearly all of our ministers work as evangelists in new fields. In the winter they go out into the churches, halls, or school houses and raise up believers. In the summer we use tents, pitching them in the cities and villages where we teach the people these doctrines. This year we shall run about 100 tents in this way. Besides these, we send out large numbers of colporters with our tracts and books, who visit the families and teach them the Bible. Last year we employed about 125 in this manner. Bible reading is another class of work. The workers go from house to house holding Bible readings with from one to twenty individuals. Last year they gave 10,000 of such Bible readings. At the same time we had employed about 300 canvassers, constantly canvassing the country and selling our larger works. In addition to this every church has a missionary society. Last year these numbered 10,500 members. Every one of these members does more or less missionary work, such as selling books, loaning or giving away tract, obtaining subscriptions to our periodicals, visiting families, looking after the poor, aiding the sick, etc. Last year they made*

31

*102,000 visits, wrote 40,000 letters, obtained 38,700*
*subscriptions to our periodicals, distributed 15,500,000*
*pages of reading matter and 1,600,000 periodicals.*

What exciting times to live in. The message was going out in a variety of ways. Everyone was active and had some part in putting this Good News that Jesus is coming out to the people. The church was growing and impacting its world.

But this didn't last forever. The first 37 years after the General Conference is formed the church grows fast. However, around the turn of the century we see a church who is getting a little more comfortable. Noticing how large it has grown, the church begins to turn inward. The reasoning seems logical. *If we don't take care of the people who are with us, we will lose them. What good is it to get more people if we are losing the ones we have?*

It seems like a logical solution. Instead of working on aggressive advancement the thinking begins to change to protecting what we have. *Strengthen the members* seems to be the way of thinking.

But as we will see there is a fallacy in this sort of thinking. The best way to strengthen members is to engage them in active service. Just as our physical bodies need exercise, so our spiritual lives do too. Instead of exercise the church, though meaning well, begins to focus on feeding the members rather than aggressive service. Though it is a slow drift it has its affect. Feeding is good, we need it, but without exercise serious problems result.

Ellen White, one of the early pioneers, saw the church was drifting away from the New Testament model of ministry. As the 1900's came she penned these words to the church:

*God has not given His ministers the work of setting the churches right. No sooner is this work done, apparently, than it has to be done over again. Church members that are thus looked after and labored for become religious weaklings. If nine tenths of the effort that has been put forth for those who know the truth had been put forth for those who have never heard the truth, how much greater would have been the advancement made! God has withheld His blessings because His people have not worked in harmony with His directions.[11]*

As she comes back to the United States from Australia she sees what is happening in the church. The churches

_____

[11] Testimonies for the Church Vol. 7, p.18

philosophy is becoming, "Strengthen the members, make sure they are theologically correct, then let them tell the world." But true strength comes from spiritual exercise. Church growth begins to stunt.

She goes on with her warnings:

*It weakens those who know the truth for our ministers to expend on them the time and talent that should be given to the unconverted . . . So long as church members make no effort to give to others the help given them, great spiritual feebleness must result.*

*The greatest help that can be given our people is to teach them to work for God, and to depend on Him, not on the ministers. Let them learn to work as Christ worked. Let them join His army of workers to do faithful service for Him.*

*There are times when it is fitting for our ministers to give on the Sabbath, in our churches, short discourses, full of the life and love of Christ. But the church members are not to expect a sermon every Sabbath.*[12]

What we consider normal she considered unfaithful. Her words were prophetic. The church chose to spend its

---

[12] Testimonies for the Church Vol. 7, pp 18,19

resources on itself and we lost many which we could have had among us.

It's staggering to think what our comfort has cost in missed opportunity. Spending our staff resources on ourselves has resulted in a growth rate of 1.74% last year. There is strong evidence that spending our staff salaries on those outside the church could have given us 8.9% growth rate. That's 7.1% growth lost in opportunity cost, or 71,000 people per year in North America. It's nice to be comfortable. It's even nicer see lost people find Jesus.

Maybe you are convinced we need to *fire* the pastors from the churches and send them out to the world. Maybe you are not. I've heard several objections to moving to a New Testament missional model of ministry. Most are legitimate questions, while a few are just excuses for being comfortable. Before we get to the key components of moving to a missional model let's deal with some of these questions people raise.

# Chapter 4

## Objections, or Why We Should Bury Our Talents.

Any time we talk about change, objections are raised. Some are legitimate questions from people who are open, but don't see the whole picture. There are others who don't want to change and are merely looking for a good excuse not to. No one will or can give the second group enough evidence. But for those who have some honest questions this chapter contains answers to a few common ones.

### *Lack of leadership*

The first obstacle that stops mission centered church is a lack of qualified leaders. There are at least three reasons for this.

One of the most challenging areas of growth I have found is leadership. It is much easier to work with objects or ideas than to work with people. It takes time to cast a

37

vision, organize a team, and help everyone move forward towards a goal. But over time a person gets better at anything they do. One begins to find ways to communicate, organize, and build. It's an amazing process to watch a leader develop.

Because of this investment of time and energy, I've found there is a danger of thinking I'm something special. When I look back and remember what God put me through to make me *usable*, I'm tempted to think I have skills no one else can develop.

A second reason leaders are not developed is a lack of self-confidence. As a leader I am so busy with my own development I don't think I have anything to give. I don't think I've learned enough yet to come along side someone and teach them how to lead.

A third scenario that comes into mind, although few would admit it is the principle of supply and demand. If I have a certain skill set and no one else in my church has this skill set, I will be more valuable to the organization. I will gain much of the praise and my job will be secure. These leaders may talk about training others, but really don't want to because it means they are less valuable. This can be a real problem because it closes down the avenues of leadership development. If new leaders are not developed the organization as a whole suffers, but the leaders already in control become more valuable (we'll question this assumption in a moment)

Yet despite these challenges a missional church must have many leaders. The importance of leadership development can be illustrated in the story of General Electric (GE). Today GE is the second largest company in the world. But they didn't start out that way. It was formed in 1892 by a merger led by J.P Morgan. In 1956 they established the "John F. Welsh Leadership Development Center." It's a 53 acre campus designed to create great leaders for the many businesses GE now runs. GE spends over 1 billion dollars on leadership training and learning for their employees each year.

Why would a company create a campus just to train it's leaders? Why would they spend so much money on leadership development? Because everything rises and falls on leadership. Whether someone is given the official title of leader, or whether they naturally become the leader of a group, to get anything done in a group requires leadership.

Today, a large part due to their emphasis on leadership training, GE makes 89 billion a year in profits. Their investment has paid off. Someone once quipped, "GE loses more good leaders each year than most companies see in a lifetime."

It's a natural reaction to keep one's own skills protected. Trade unions do this all the time. But when it means the mission suffers and the kingdom of God is smaller, it's not worth it.

Jesus disciples struggled with self-preservation. They argued up to the night of His betrayal who would be the greatest. Jesus had to stoop down and wash their feet to show them in His kingdom the greatest is the least.

Let me challenge you, a person who can teach another person skills you have, with a new paradigm of what value is.

Imagine an island with a hundred people who live there. These people are poor. Each one has to work all day just to farm enough food to eat that day. All their energy is used to get enough food for one day's survival. This leaves no time for anything else. Work, eat, and the day is over.

One day a man (we'll call him Al), just by chance finds some seeds that when planted, yield ten days of food for the efforts of one day's work. He is excited by this discovery. Soon he has food to spare.

He discovers he can trade this food for labor. People are willing to work one day for one day's worth of food instead of farming it themselves.

Al finds this exciting. Now he can work one day for food, keep one day's worth for himself and trade the rest away. He decides to add on to his hut, make it really nice. So he hires nine people to work on this while he farms the food for them.

It's a great discovery. Now 99 people are raising 99 days of food each day, and one person is producing 10 days of food each day. The production of the island has gone up to 109 units (99+10) of food each day from 100. By Al's discovery the total island production is up 9%! This helps the islands economy and enriches everyone on average, although Al is receiving most the benefits.

One day Al is thinking about this. He would like to share his seeds with everyone else. It would help others produce more. But Al is afraid if he shares his secret, others won't need to come to him for food and he will be a poor man again. If everyone else is producing 10 days of food each day, no one else will trade him work for food and his house will not get as big as he would like it to be.

This perplexes Al for several months. But as he sees his house getting bigger and everyone else struggle along, guilt finally overwhelms him and he shares seeds with everyone else on the island. He resigns himself to being poor again just like everyone else. The scarcity power he had is gone.

It's a great moral lesson about doing right and caring about others even if it hurts you. Al gets points for unselfishness. But what is the end result?

The islander's each are able to produce ten days worth of food every day. Now the economy is producing 1,000 units of food per day (100 x 10). What will they do with all the extra food?

What is not immediately apparent to Al is that by sharing he hasn't lost as much as he thinks. At first he thinks he has. There are no worker's who want to trade food for working on his house because they are all excited about planting their own gardens. This depresses Al and he thinks maybe he made the wrong choice. He goes to his garden and works to get his ten days of food. He comes home and stores it because there is no one to sell it to. *I guess I'll just have to eat it* he thinks. He goes to bed and in the morning gets ready to go to the garden. But wait, he still has nine days of food left. Why go to the garden?

Then he has a eureka moment. He has the next nine days that he doesn't have to work for food. He can work on his own house for nine days. He does and is better off than he thought. In fact Al now becomes a carpenter and finds in his new profession the payment he can receive for a days worth of labor is exactly ten days of food. The amount of food he would receive if he farmed it. Supply and demand make wages equal throughout the island. Now he is no worse off than when he kept the new seeds to himself, and his neighbors are ten times better off without hurting Al's lifestyle.

There was a period in the 16$^{th}$ to 18$^{th}$ century where economically, Al's first philosophy pervaded. It is called mercantilism. People thought there was only so much wealth in the world, so if you have it that means I can't. However, people like Adam Smith showed the world that wealth has to do with production. If you produce great value, that doesn't limit me from also producing great value. My wealth doesn't limit your wealth. We both can do well if we both produce valuable products or services.

Sometimes as leaders we can think like Al. I'll keep these skills to myself so that I can keep my power, influence, job, etc. But we don't realize by training someone with all the knowledge we have, we lose nothing. If you owned a business and you needed leaders to open new franchises, who would be more valuable to you? A leader who could open a franchise or a person who could train someone to be a leader who could open a franchise? I would take a trainer any day because if I have the trainer, I can create the leaders.

As church members it's important understand this thinking. We need to train leaders to create new groups and ministries within the church and start new churches. We really can't have too many. Good leaders can respect the skills of someone else and step down for a while and let someone else lead. It's only the non-producing, mercantile leaders who can't.

So the challenge to each of us is to share skills. Don't worry if you don't have everything figured out. Don't fall into the trap of thinking no one else can learn the skills you have. Teach with grace and encouragement. Make your joy, not having the skills, but seeing how fast your student is learning. That's the mark of your true value.

## *Upset people*

Another objection to true mission structure is voiced by concerned people whose heart is in the right place. The argument goes something like this: *Yes, you are right. The structure we operate under is not God's plan for his church. But if we change now we will make people upset. In fact, changing the structure could be so unsettling we could split the church.*

Others argue along the same lines that if we upset too many people they will get mad and people will stop supporting the church with tithes and offerings. The financial resources of the church will dry up, then we will have no way to support mission anyway, so it is better not to rock the boat, use the system we have and do what we can with the resources we have.

I hear the point. It is made by legitimately concerned people. But there are parts of the picture such an argument doesn't consider.

First, we have to remember the mission of Jesus' church. Remember the reason he established it? – to seek and to save the lost, and make those lost people into Jesus disciples. Anything that damages the church's ability to do its mission must be changed.

We have to ask, what are we really risking? It's true that we may lose members. It's also true we may lose financial resources. Where we make a mistake is to make an assumption this is bad.

I don't want to see anyone leave the church. My hope is that everyone can be a part of God's mission and experience the joy of being a part of something significant in their life – connecting people with Jesus. But if someone comes to a point where they care so much about themselves and so little about the lost they would choose to withdraw their financial support and even membership because the church is serious about lost people, should we spend the resources of the church (whose mission is to reach the lost) to cater to their whims?

When people leave a church that decides to put its resources towards reaching the lost, it is not the structural change that makes them leave. The structural change merely highlights the dysfunction that is already present. When a church decides to restructure for mission it doesn't lose members who care about the lost, it only looses members who care about themselves.

We are all growing. I care about selfish people too. We all struggle with selfishness. I want everyone to be in the church. But we have a choice to make. Are we going to spend our resources on those who have experienced Jesus, or those who haven't? The story of the shepherd who leaves the ninety-nine sheep in the fold and goes after one who is lost makes it clear which one's Jesus wants us to spend our time on.[13]

---

[13] Luke 15:3-7

It seems like a cruel choice. Leave those who have supported the church. But we have to see the whole picture. Every dollar we spend on the saved is one we can't spend on the lost. Every hour of time we spend on the saved is one we can't spend on the lost. The cost of missing the opportunity is bigger than many would like to admit. It's like working at McDonald's for $10 an hour when you have the opportunity of working construction for $25. The cost of choosing to work at McDonalds is actually $15 an hour, since you are foregoing the other opportunity. You may think you are doing well, but in light of the bigger picture, we see there is a better choice. We do the same by concentrating resources on the sheep in the fold.

It is crucial to realize we should never stop structural change for mission because of those who withdraw membership or finances from the church. To do so sacrifices mission and sustains a dysfunctional structure.

Some would argue if we don't do anything to stop the disgruntled from leaving the church, their salvation could be at stake. I would urge a missional model will do more for true spiritually and therefore the security of members salvation than the standard model today.

I hope you see the issues at stake when we give in to people who are upset about changes to reach the lost.

We also need to understand financial concerns are not as big as we may think. First, much of the churches resources are being spent on members. If we lost members we'd loose these resources, but only a small percentage of these lost resources are being spent on lost people anyway. Most are used to pay a pastor to minister to the members.

Second, a model where the pastor is the church planter and trainer for the area, then lets elders run the church, takes a lot less resources! Only a fraction. It's always nice to have extra church planters in a district. But even if we lose half our resources we'd be better off. Because the pastors would be planting churches which know it's their job to run the church as an outreach center.

The real risk is compromising mission rather than losing members or resources.

## *The power of a paycheck*

When we think about turning leadership of the local church over to the elders, a very real concern arises. There have been times when local elders have made power plays to take over the church from a pastor. Among them are those whose theological understanding is less than ideal. This can be a real problem when those who misunderstand the Gospel want to take over the leadership of the church.

Now and then even a paid pastor will come up with an idea that is not really founded in the Bible and take a church away from the truth of the Bible. In this case there is a cure built into the system. The pastor gets a paycheck. If there is a serious problem the conference can solve it by cutting off this paycheck. Of course most conferences I know will first attempt to work with the pastor trying to solve differences. But if nothing helps there is the solution to fire the pastor.

However, what if elders run the local church? You can't fire a volunteer can you? Local elders are elected by the church vote through a nominating committee. So the situation could develop where an elder who is teaching erroneous doctrine could still have enough influence to be elected year after year, spreading false gospel. If the church has no pastor, who is going to take care of the problem? We end up with a bunch of congregations believing different "truths" all under the banner of the Seventh-day Adventist Church.

This is something our founders were afraid of. They wanted some structure to protect truth. Some way of constantly moving us towards more truth, rather than splintering over disagreements. If we remove the pastors how can we deal with this?

How did the New Testament Christians deal with it? They did leave the church in the hands of local elders. They took that risk for the sake of mission.

There are two ways they kept the faith pure. First, they were much more mission minded. Everyone had a piece of the mission. When your life is spent on mission you tend to stay more focused on truth. There are exceptions, but as a general rule it's true.

Second, they did something we don't do. They appointed the local elders. Never in the New Testament is an elder elected. Deacons are elected (their job is to serve the churches needs). Elders are always appointed by what we would call today the district pastor, or the paid clergy.

Notice again what Paul tells Titus:

*The reason I left you in Crete was that you might straighten out what was left unfinished and appoint elders in every town, as I directed you. Titus 1:5*

Can you see the reason elders are appointed? It accomplishes the same thing as paying a pastor does –

only it costs a lot less. If the paid district pastor appoints elders in each church, if there is a problem, the paid district pastor can remove them. Just like a paycheck, if worse comes to worse something can be done.

Of course, the pastor who appoints the elders may take the advice of some of the church members as to who they see as good candidates for the job of elder. But setting it up this way leaves a solution if there is a problem. The paid pastor, who we are beginning to realize takes more of an apostle role, can step in and remove an elder if there is a major problem. The New Testament gives that authority of appointing elders.

I know this makes some uncomfortable. It is not the way we've done it in the Adventist church recently, but it is how they did it in New Testament times. And it worked.

This biblical method creates a balance of power that holds all of us responsible for mission. The congregations choose deacons and others to serve them. The paid district pastors choose the elders. The conference hires the pastors, and the church members elect the conference administration. It creates a balanced loop where all of us are being held accountable, and are holding others accountable for mission. And if it means we stay focused and more people are saved in the kingdom, well, that's really good news!

# Chapter 5

# How to Do Church Without a Pastor

So what does a church look like without a pastor? Is it the same picture but with elders leading instead of pastors? At the risk of challenging the traditional thinking a little more, let's paint that picture.

The reason the church exists is to make disciples.[14] The rest of what happens at church is secondary. So to be true to this Great Commission, this needs to be our number one goal. If we keep this first thing first, the rest of what we need (like fellowship) will happen. In fact, my experience tells me true fellowship and camaraderie cannot happen unless we are all straining towards the same goal. Military minds around the world understand if they put a group of people together, under the stresses of battle there is a closeness that develops in no other way. They use this to

---

[14] Matthew 28:19-20

their advantage. People who may not die for their nation will die for their comrades.

We can have this same closeness even in church, but it happens under the strain of doing all we can together to make disciples. True fellowship flows from focus on this goal.

So faithfulness to Jesus Commission compels us to design church in a way that is the most effective way to make disciples. I may prefer one kind of church where I am comfortable, I know everybody, I don't have to get my life all messy with people who have problems. But Jesus reminds us that church is not about "I". "I" am one of the ninty-nine sheep safe in the fold. It's about the one who is lost.[15]

So how do we design a church where we can make the most disciples with the least effort. How can we get the most out of what we put in? If we are happy in church the way it is, this is a hard question to ask. But if we really care about that lost one it's a question we must ask.

It would be a hard question to answer except we have an extensive record of those who made disciples in the New Testament. And the record we find there suggests the

---

[15] Luke 15:1-7

solution is for the church to get smaller so it can get bigger.

Consider the following inspired record.

**Romans 16:5** Please give my greetings to the church that *meets in their home.* Greet my dear friend Epenetus. He was the very first person to become a Christian in the province of Asia.

**Romans 16:23** Gaius says hello to you. I am his guest, and *the church meets here in his home.* Erastus, the city treasurer, sends you his greetings, and so does Quartus, a Christian brother.

**1 Corinthians 16:19** The churches here in the province of Asia greet you heartily in the Lord, along with Aquila and Priscilla and all the others who gather *in their home for church meetings.*

**Colossians 4:15** Please give my greetings to our Christian brothers and sisters at Laodicea, and to Nympha and those who *meet in her house.*

**Philemon 1:1-3** This letter is from Paul, … *I am also writing to the church that meets in your house.* May

God our Father and the Lord Jesus Christ give you grace and peace.[16]

The New Testament method to make disciples is by using "house churches". Today we would call these small groups. I actually prefer the name Milton Adam uses because it's descriptive of why they exist. He calls them Growth Groups.

There were once three thousand converted in a day.[17] Did you ever wonder how the church was able to absorb that many new converts? They didn't build an auditorium that seated three thousand. They absorbed the new converts through groups that met in members' homes. The New Testament writers called these groups churches.

If the purpose of the church really is to make disciples, and the secondary goal is to fellowship, then this is significant because true discipleship (and true fellowship) cannot really happen in a group much above thirteen. Thirteen is the "church" size Jesus used.

Here's why small is critical and why I believe Jesus limited His group to thirteen.

---

[16] http://www.adamsonline.org/SimpleChurch/SimpleChurch_page000 3.htm

[17] Acts 2:41

To get a grasp of how just a few extra people change the dynamics of a group consider the relationships in a room.

If you and I are the only people in a room there is just one relationship in the room, the one between you and me. That's a pretty intimate setting where we can talk about important things and know we have the full attention of the other.

Now consider a friend joins us. Now there are two more relationships. Not only is there a relationship between you and I, but also we each have a relationship with the new person for a total of three. The *energy* in the room just tripled.

When a fourth person walks in she adds three more relationships (one with each person already in the room) to make six. As more people join, the *energy* or feel of the room grows, not by one, but how many relationships they add to the room. At twelve there are sixty-six relationships and at thirteen (the size of Jesus church) there are seventy-eight.[18] By adding only five people to thirteen we get a

---

[18] The formula to find the number of relationships in a group is number of people in the group times one less than the number in the group all divided by two.

hundred and fifty-three relationships, almost double what we had at thirteen.

Why does this matter? Because it's important to understand that adding just a few more people than what Jesus modeled changes the whole group. Big gatherings may be good for other reasons, but discipleship and fellowship only happen in a close, safe, nurturing environment. Going much above Jesus example means sacrificing discipleship and fellowship for something else. Yet, we can't sacrifice discipleship because the church exists to make disciples.

As startling as it may be, if the main meeting of the "church" is a group much larger than the thirteen modeled by Jesus we really can't call it church – at least not a church built on the Bible. Because the church built on the Bible is about making disciples, and Jesus example shows us disciples are made in small groups where close relationships can develop.

At this point you may feel challenged with your concept of church. As I started to realize how different most current churches are from the biblical model I felt challenged too. Could we really be that far off base? But as I studied it became clear most of what is done in the name of church is not church.

Please don't misunderstand, I believe God fearing people with good motives were behind what we have. Many of those we have to thank for our current "church" were honest people trying to do what they could for God. Let us not criticize their motives. Like Martin Luther, or John Calvin they were inspired and used by God. However, humans, even ones with true motives make mistakes. Let's honor men and women who went before us for their faithfulness to God, but let's not be so awed by their good deeds we make their mistakes sacred. To do so would not honor the God they honored.

The picture of church begins to come clear. Church is the small group that meets in homes. That is where discipleship and fellowship take place. Neither can truly take place in a big group. However, that doesn't rule out owning a building or renting a place to meet. Ellen White, one of the early pioneers of the Adventist Church saw the advantage of a place to meet to lend stability to new converts[19]. After all, in her day pastors would move on to plant more churches. There is a place for church buildings. But the essence of church is the small group that meets in homes.

---

[19] Testimonies for the Church Vol 6 pp.100-101

Ellen White goes so far as to say:

*The Formation of small companies as a basis of Christian effort has been presented to me by One who cannot err.*[20]

Before we move on to the next chapter consider six reasons your church should organize around small churches or growth groups.

## *Discipleship can happen*

As we've already said, true discipleship can't happen in a group bigger than what Jesus modeled. Jesus is a smart guy, we really can't do better . . .

## *Fellowship can happen*

The result of discipleship is fellowship. When discipleship happens, so does fellowship. Small group church creates an atmosphere for fellowship.

---

[20] Testimonies for the Church Vol 7, pp. 21,22

### Develops Leaders

Each group has two co-leaders that will grow stronger and wiser over time. As the group church grows bigger than thirteen, it multiplies itself. Each co-leader takes part of the group so it can continue to grow. This allows each new leader to train another co-leader. This not only creates capable leaders, but it helps the Adventist Church with a major issue we have. Two-thirds of our membership are women. I praise God for every decision for God that has been made by a man or woman. However, it seems that we are doing church in a way that doesn't appeal to men as much.

Men are more hands on and active. (Just watch little boys and girls play.) Giving more opportunity for leadership involvement not only makes the church stronger by developing more leaders, but it also helps with the inner need of many men to do something.

### Allows one "church building" to minister to many people

God has put many kinds of people on this earth. Even within one community there are rich and poor, educated and not. People think differently from each other. We see

61

this most strikingly in worship styles, and especially music. Now I'm not so naive as to think small groups will solve all the music issues. However, if someone is part of a group with people who think like they do and they can trust, they will be less likely to leave over worship styles.

## Pastoral care is done better than any paid clergy ever could

Imagine a pastor with a church of one hundred people. This pastor, because of other commitments can only visit one member per day, five days a week. So he goes about his visits. Every twenty weeks each member is visited for 90 minutes.

Now consider a second pastor with a church of one hundred. But this church has ten groups with ten members each. They meet to share life for 90 minutes each week, but the paid pastor doesn't visit at all.

Who is more cared for? The members who see their pastor for 90 minutes every twenty weeks, or the members who in a sense have a group of nine other pastors every week for 90 minutes?

## *Research has already been done to find proven ways groups can work*

When we think about small groups becoming the essence of church, we are not talking about some theory. Research has been done and it's been proven to work.

The best material have found on the nuts and bolts of small group church is written by an Adventist pastor by the name of Milton Adams. Pastor Adams has been working on the details of how to do this for twenty years and has ironed out many of the wrinkles of how to get back to this biblical model. The best part of it all is he offers his material free (at the time of this writing) to anyone who wants to use it. You can go to his website at www.GrowthGroups.us and download videos, a training manual, and a host of other material. His materials are also available through www.AdventSource.com. I highly recommend you use this resource. It is what I use and it works!

# Chapter 6

## How to Get Rid of Israel's King

It's one thing to talk about changing structure for
mission. It's another to do it. Here are five steps to moving
to a mission centered ministry model.

### Communicate the problem

The Adventist Church is full of good people. People
who want to do what is right and desire to know God's
truth whatever the personal cost to them. I feel privileged
to be a part of this movement I believe God has led and
directed. But that doesn't mean we haven't made mistakes
along the way. Israel, who were God's chosen people for
the purpose of mission, got to places in their history they
worshipped Baal, a god of sex and human sacrifice. Were
they still God's chosen people? Amazingly, yes! Their sin
caused a lot of misery as sin always does, but God didn't
abandon them. Praise God for His grace.

The problem is not a lack of good people, the problem
is many of our people don't realize the cost our current

structure has incurred. I believe hundreds of millions of people have been missed because of our current structure.

The first key to a missional structure is to communicate the problem. If our members don't see the urgency and cost of the same routine they will think change is too much trouble. But if they understand where we are and the true cost, the Holy Spirit can move on their hearts to reach the lost. Antoine de Saint-Exupery once said,

*"If you want to build a ship, don't herd people together to collect wood and don't assign them tasks and work, but rather teach them to long for the endless immensity of the sea."*

Communicating the problem will go a long way to awaken the need in the hearts of our people. You can do this by sharing some of the information in this book. You can get a free pdf copy online at 101.church.

There are also other books you can share. A classic, which convinced me that a mission centered structure is crucial is *Revolution in the Church* by Russell Burrill. It is a passionate plea for healthy mission focus.

It is also important this whole process includes the pastor. Most pastors I know would love to spend more time with the lost. Many burn out trying to meet the needs of the members, which really are never satisfied until members themselves get involved in reaching the lost and misguided. It's a never-ending, unrewarding cycle I've been a part of. If you offer to turn your pastor loose to spend nine-tenths of his or her time with the lost, most likely something deep inside will awake and you will see a new person who is excited about life.

## *Introduce small groups*

A critical part of the process of changing structure is creating another structure that can sustain the church. As has already been discussed, small groups create that structure. I recommend the material found at www.GrowthGroups.us to do this.

## *Talk to the conference*

After communicating to the church the need for structural change and creating a small group structure for support, the next step is to talk to the local conference. The local conference is the interpreter of the church manual and has the authority to allow a church to set aside the normal rules, especially when moving to a model that more accurately reflects the biblical precedence.[21] We are all on the same team. It's important to communicate to the conference the reason you want to change structure is for mission.

Sometimes people get this idea that it's us against them, the conference versus the church. This is absurd since the conference administration is elected by the local churches. Ultimately, it's the combined will of the local churches that determines who the conference leadership is. We are all on the same team. Most conference administrators are happy to help the local church reach the lost better. That's why they are there.

So step three, talk to the conference. Brainstorm ways to put this New Testament model into practice. You will see a church and a pastor change.

## *Define the elder's role*

As we've said already, a key step in this process is making clear the elders role in the local church. They are the overseers of the church. This is the New Testament job

---

[21] The Seventh-day Adventist Church manual allows for variance from its direction under certain circumstances. p.2

description. The word "presbuteros" used for elder in the New Testament literally means guardian, or overseer. That's why 1 Timothy 3 and Titus 1 give such clear characteristics for a district pastor to look for in an elder. They have both an awesome privilege and responsibility.

Because of this responsibility elders have to make tough decisions. Decisions not everyone will like or agree with. So the New Testament gives two guidelines to protect them.

First, they can't be voted out of office. The district pastor appoints them. They can be removed if there is a real problem. However, if they've merely stood for truth and someone doesn't like it there is a buffer.

Second, Paul tells Timothy in 1 Timothy 5:19

*"Do not entertain an accusation against an elder unless it is brought by two or three witnesses"*

People may complain about elders if they are doing a good job. Paul says, don't even waste your time listening to complaints about the elders you've appointed unless more than one person has the same complaint." Because of the important position an elder holds it is vital that they be protected. If they are not, the mission and theology of the local church could be determined by whoever complains the loudest.

When you redefine the elders' role it's important to build these two principles of protection into the structure so the elders can do the job they are meant to do.

Exactly how each church uses their elders is flexible. The main key is that they are the overseers of the church. I've found it works well to appoint four elders. One to be in charge of Worship, one Outreach, one Discipleship or growth groups, and one Administration. Every area of church life should fall under one of these categories.

It's also important to appoint a head elder from one of the four, or appoint five and make one of them head elder. Again, the structure can be flexible as long as they are fulfilling the job of overseer.

Notice the New Testament does NOT say an elder's job is to preach, or to have a prayer on Sabbath, or even to visit the sick. Many times we have crippled our churches by thinking only elders can do these things. The natural place for visiting and pastoral care to happen is in the growth group. An elder may have one of these gifts and do them, but it's not the job of elder to preach or pray, or visit the sick. It's their job to make sure that the church stays on the course of mission.

Is it important who preaches or teaches on Sabbath? Sure. But teaching or preaching is not automatically an elder gift. If a church decides to divide overseeing into the four areas mentioned it would be the Worship Overseers job to make sure there are good services. But it's not their job or the other elder's job to do all the preaching.

Do you begin to see the picture? God gives all different spiritual gifts to members. When each member uses their spiritual gift the church has all it needs to be strong. The elder's job is more to help others be the best they can be and find a place in ministry then to do all the ministry themselves. This uses the spiritual gifts God has given the whole church rather than those of just a few.

It's exciting to think of a church fully employed with the gifts God gives. And it's the correct understanding of the elder's role that supports the development of gifts in everyone else. If we don't understand the elder's role and the paid pastor's role, we will never be able to use the spiritual gifts of the rest of the members to their full potential.

## Renegotiate the pastor's role

Just as critical as defining the elder's role in the church is defining the paid pastor's role. This may take more effort, not because it takes a bigger stretch of thinking, but because it involves more people. Many pastors have more than one church. For the pastor to truly be able to function in the biblical role requires all churches and the local conference to understand and agree to the plan. Again, communication is important.

There are four keys to help the pastor minister in the New Testament way and avoid the temptation of mission drift.

I discovered the first one when the conference I work for made some district changes. Instead of defining my district as the churches I pastor, they redefined the districts by zip codes. What this did was give every paid pastor a certain territory they were responsible to reach.

Before the redistricting it was easy for me to think of the towns between the next pastor and I as his responsibility. After all, I am busy serving the members of the church. He should reach those towns. By defining districts by zip codes I can't pass responsibility off on someone else. If the paid pastor and people in this district don't make an effort to reach those towns they will not be reached. The responsibility rests on us.

This simple redistricting creates a whole new thinking about ministry. It shows just how selfish it is to demand a paid pastor over each church while people all around are dying out of a saving relationship with Jesus. Our comfort costs lost people.

The next two keys deal with the pastor's role. In *Testimonies for the Church Vol 7, page 18* there is an interesting statement Ellen White makes about the paid pastor's role. The whole section is worth reading. Notice the ratio of time with church versus time with lost people she suggests.

> *God has not given His ministers the work of setting the churches right. No sooner is this work done, apparently, than it has to be done over again. Church members that are thus looked after and labored for become religious weaklings. If **nine-tenths** of the effort that has been put forth for those who know the truth had been put forth for those who have never heard the truth, how much greater would have been the advancement made! God has withheld His blessings*

*because His people have not worked in harmony with His directions.*

The argument is many times made, *Let's get ourselves to the spiritual state we need to be so we can go out and tell the world about Jesus.* But the truth is, we will never get to the spiritual state we need to be *until* we tell the world about Jesus. We are spending thousands of dollars each month in salaries to create weak members.

But notice the suggestion she gives. Nine-tenths on the lost, one tenth on the saved. If a paid pastor works 40 hours in one week, only 4 hours should be spent with the saved. That's barely enough time to show up for church! As you read this section of the Testimonies we begin to understand early Adventism had a very different view of ministry, and we see why they grew over four times faster than we are.

The new role of the paid pastor should be to spend 36 hours a week reaching out to places other can't. If he or she reaches out to places church members can, he or she takes away the members role, and weakens the members. When a child is learning to walk we must let them fall and get up again. The child will never learn to walk until we turn them loose.

This frees up someone to work almost full time starting new ministries in the district. This is important since most members don't have the amount of time a new church plant requires. But it also creates in the district someone who knows how to reach the lost. If someone spends 36 hours a week running the church soon they will become good at it. But if they spend 36 hours reaching the lost and starting new ministries they will become good at that. If you want to learn how to reach the lost, would you rather learn from someone who does it 36 hours a week or four hours a week? The guy who does it 36 hours a week will know about nine times more about it.

So the second role of the paid pastor is to come back to the churches in the district and teach four hours a week. And since he knows so much more about outreach these sessions become very powerful times of teaching.

So first, create districts geographically. This refocuses the church and helps everyone see the situation clearly. Second, make the paid pastor's main job to reach the lost in places others can't (essentially a church planter). Third, have this now expert evangelist come back and teach 1/10th of the time.

## *Conclusion*

The preceding five steps are not all that could be said about structural change. Understanding spiritual gifts is important. We haven't even talked about worker's going out two by two, which is standard in the New Testament.

More discussion needs to be done on the topic. But as we move ahead in a direction we know God has called us to go He will show us the way. When we take one step He will show us the next, until looking back the whole path becomes clear and we will see God's leading all along.

*The harvest truly is great, but the laborers are few. Earnestly beg the Lord of the harvest to throw out workers into the harvest field.* Luke 10:2[22]

Will you join me in this prayer Jesus asks us to pray? And give Him permission to start with you?

---

[22] Thanks to Dr. Derek Morris for illuminating this text for me.

# Chapter 7

## A Final Word To Those About to Be Fired

I remember the first call the Holy Spirit put on my heart to be a pastor. It was a special time as God showed me what my life work would be. I received my Bachelor's degree in Theology and headed off to the Seminary for more training. Then it was finally time for full time ministry.

Those first few months of full time ministry were glorious ones. I was ready to change the world and I knew God was with me and would help me do it.

But as time went on I found myself spending less time changing the world and more time trying to change the church. I had a sense that bringing lost people to the church would not be helpful in its present condition. So I preached sermons to grow the saints.

There were few gains. As Ellen White observed in the passage we looked at earlier, *no sooner is this work done, apparently, than it has to be done over again.* I found myself in an endless cycle of trying to get the church in a condition to reach the lost. I always hoped to spend more time reaching the lost, and I would be able to, just as soon as the church was in the right condition. That day never came. I realize now it never can come until the structure we minister under changes.

This frustration drove me to a deep desire to plant a church. If we begin a new church with the idea every member is expected to be involved in outreach then maybe there is hope to reach the world. So I set out to design a church where every member is a minister and the church doesn't depend on paid pastoral support.

Taking a step of faith I quit my job and traveled across the country to carry out this dream. I found a new job as a real estate agent believing God could help my family and I live off commissions if He wanted to. Five months later we found ourselves out of money and wondering why God did not come through. If it were not for help from some good people we wouldn't have lasted that long.

I had a lot of questions then. Isn't God the same powerful God as the days of the Bible? Couldn't He have supported us? Why didn't He?

Out of desperation I again took a job as a pastor. But this time the conference was taking some bold steps for mission. In the first few months they decided to redefine the districts by zip code. This changed everything.

Now I could see clearly my responsibility. It wasn't to the churches in my district. They only existed to reach the 285,000 people in our zipcodes. When you know your objective things become clear.

Now, out of necessity, it was important to appoint local elders over the established churches so I could start new ministries. Now I could clearly communicate to the members of the churches what we are giving up for comfort. No one else would reach our territory if we didn't.

Some grumbled, but many could see what it cost to demand a pastor each week. Even though they preferred to have a paid pastor every week they gave that up for mission. Their willingness to sacrifice for mission still amazes me.

This is an ongoing process and we are still learning. I work as hard as I ever have but now I'm actually making a difference in the world.

I wonder how many pastors have quit because of this seeming inability to make a difference? According to a 1998 survey done by *Focus on the Family*, ". . .1,500 pastors leave their assignments each month, due to moral failure, spiritual burnout or contention within their local congregations."[23]

Can you blame them? If it were not for the courageous actions of certain conference officials who were willing to take some risks on mission I would be one of these casualties.

I find more fulfillment now then I ever have because I work under a structure I can actually make a lasting difference.

I am excited where our church is going. We have major issues ahead. But despite awesome challenges leadership is seeing these challenges and facing them. There is major change ahead. It will take courage and wisdom to finish getting the message out, just like it did when the Adventist Church started getting the message out. But by being open to the Holy Spirit's moving, and following the biblical structure they got that message out and so will we.

---

[23] http://www2.focusonthefamily.com/docstudy/newsletters/A0000008
03.cfm

# Appendix A

The following table lists growth rates of the Adventist Church by year. To be exact it is 8.91677%. From 1863 this percentage is added to the next year and so on until we get to 1900. This has the affect of compounding membership yearly. You will notice in 1900 both the projected growth and the actual growth is the same number. This confirms that the average growth rate of just over 8.9% is indeed the average for the first 37 years of the Adventist Church.

### Table of actual and projected growth 1863 to 1900[24]

| Year | Members | Annual growth | Average growth at 8.9% |
|------|---------|---------------|------------------------|
| 1863 | 3,500   |               | 3,500                  |
| 1864 | 3,800   | 8.57%         | 3,812                  |
| 1865 | 4,000   | 5.26%         | 4,152                  |
| 1866 | 4,250   | 6.25%         | 4,522                  |
| 1867 | 4,320   | 1.65%         | 4,925                  |
| 1868 | 4,475   | 3.59%         | 5,365                  |
| 1869 | 4,900   | 9.50%         | 5,843                  |

---

[24] www.AdventistStatistics.org.

| | | | |
|---|---|---|---|
| 1870 | 5,440 | 11.02% | 6,364 |
| 1871 | 4,550 | -16.36% | 6,931 |
| 1872 | 4,901 | 7.71% | 7,550 |
| 1873 | 5,875 | 19.87% | 8,223 |
| 1875 | 8,042 | 36.89% | 8,956 |
| 1876 | 10,044 | 24.89% | 9,755 |
| 1877 | 11,608 | 15.57% | 10,624 |
| 1878 | 13,077 | 12.66% | 11,572 |
| 1879 | 14,141 | 8.14% | 12,603 |
| 1880 | 15,570 | 10.11% | 13,727 |
| 1881 | 16,916 | 8.64% | 14,951 |
| 1882 | 17,169 | 1.50% | 16,284 |
| 1883 | 17,317 | 0.86% | 17,737 |
| 1884 | 18,702 | 8.00% | 19,318 |
| 1885 | 20,547 | 9.87% | 21,041 |
| 1886 | 23,111 | 12.48% | 22,917 |
| 1887 | 25,841 | 11.81% | 24,960 |
| 1888 | 26,112 | 1.05% | 27,186 |
| 1889 | 28,324 | 8.47% | 29,610 |
| 1890 | 29,711 | 4.90% | 32,250 |
| 1891 | 31,665 | 6.58% | 35,126 |
| 1892 | 33,778 | 6.67% | 38,258 |
| 1893 | 37,404 | 10.73% | 41,669 |
| 1894 | 42,763 | 14.33% | 45,385 |
| 1895 | 47,680 | 11.50% | 49,432 |
| 1896 | 52,202 | 9.48% | 53,839 |
| 1897 | 56,426 | 8.09% | 58,640 |
| 1898 | 59,347 | 5.18% | 63,869 |
| 1899 | 64,003 | 7.85% | 69,564 |
| 1900 | **75,767** | 18.38% | **75,767** |

# Appendix B

Growth trends in North America 1913 –2006

Growth since separate statistics were kept for the North American division in 1913 has been minimal. The average growth during these years is 2.916819%. The year by year data follows:

| Year | Membership | Growth Rate | Avg annual growth |
|------|-----------|-------------|-------------------|
| 1913 | 71,863 | | 71,863 |
| 1914 | 72,015 | 0.21% | 73,959 |
| 1915 | 77,735 | 7.94% | 76,116 |
| 1916 | 79,946 | 2.84% | 78,337 |
| 1917 | 87,222 | 9.10% | 80,621 |
| 1918 | 91,972 | 5.45% | 82,973 |
| 1919 | 95,645 | 3.99% | 85,393 |
| 1920 | 95,877 | 0.24% | 87,884 |
| 1921 | 98,715 | 2.96% | 90,447 |
| 1922 | 101,129 | 2.45% | 93,086 |
| 1923 | 102,797 | 1.65% | 95,801 |
| 1924 | 106,941 | 4.03% | 98,595 |
| 1925 | 108,802 | 1.74% | 101,471 |
| 1926 | 110,422 | 1.49% | 104,431 |
| 1927 | 112,276 | 1.68% | 107,477 |
| 1928 | 113,737 | 1.30% | 110,612 |
| 1929 | 117,771 | 3.55% | 113,838 |
| 1930 | 120,560 | 2.37% | 117,158 |
| 1931 | 127,787 | 5.99% | 120,576 |
| 1932 | 135,837 | 6.30% | 124,093 |
| 1933 | 143,777 | 5.85% | 127,712 |
| 1934 | 151,216 | 5.17% | 131,437 |

| | | | |
|---|---|---|---|
| 1935 | 157,507 | 4.16% | 135,271 |
| 1936 | 161,271 | 2.39% | 139,217 |
| 1937 | 164,490 | 2.00% | 143,277 |
| 1938 | 171,214 | 4.09% | 147,457 |
| 1939 | 177,341 | 3.58% | 151,758 |
| 1940 | 185,788 | 4.76% | 156,184 |
| 1941 | 191,333 | 2.98% | 160,740 |
| 1942 | 197,215 | 3.07% | 165,428 |
| 1943 | 201,111 | 1.98% | 170,253 |
| 1944 | 206,908 | 2.88% | 175,219 |
| 1945 | 212,514 | 2.71% | 180,330 |
| 1946 | 220,122 | 3.58% | 185,590 |
| 1947 | 228,179 | 3.66% | 191,004 |
| 1948 | 235,460 | 3.19% | 196,575 |
| 1949 | 243,193 | 3.28% | 202,308 |
| 1950 | 251,039 | 3.23% | 208,209 |
| 1951 | 260,185 | 3.64% | 214,283 |
| 1952 | 268,533 | 3.21% | 220,533 |
| 1953 | 275,733 | 2.68% | 226,965 |
| 1954 | 285,777 | 3.64% | 233,585 |
| 1955 | 293,448 | 2.68% | 240,399 |
| 1956 | 299,984 | 2.23% | 247,411 |
| 1957 | 308,695 | 2.90% | 254,627 |
| 1958 | 318,939 | 3.32% | 262,054 |
| 1959 | 325,882 | 2.18% | 269,698 |
| 1960 | 332,364 | 1.99% | 277,565 |
| 1961 | 343,664 | 3.40% | 285,661 |
| 1962 | 351,048 | 2.15% | 293,993 |
| 1963 | 361,878 | 3.09% | 302,568 |
| 1964 | 370,688 | 2.43% | 311,393 |
| 1965 | 380,855 | 2.74% | 320,476 |
| 1966 | 391,014 | 2.67% | 329,824 |
| 1967 | 401,970 | 2.80% | 339,444 |
| 1968 | 419,841 | 4.45% | 349,345 |
| 1969 | 426,295 | 1.54% | 359,535 |
| 1970 | 439,726 | 3.15% | 370,022 |
| 1971 | 454,096 | 3.27% | 380,815 |
| 1972 | 470,622 | 3.64% | 391,923 |
| 1973 | 486,601 | 3.40% | 403,354 |

| | | | |
|---|---|---|---|
| 1974 | 503,689 | 3.51% | 415,119 |
| 1975 | 520,842 | 3.41% | 427,228 |
| 1976 | 536,649 | 3.03% | 439,689 |
| 1977 | 551,884 | 2.84% | 452,514 |
| 1978 | 566,453 | 2.64% | 465,713 |
| 1979 | 585,050 | 3.28% | 479,297 |
| 1980 | 604,430 | 3.31% | 493,277 |
| 1981 | 622,961 | 3.07% | 507,665 |
| 1982 | 642,317 | 3.11% | 522,473 |
| 1983 | 660,253 | 2.79% | 537,713 |
| 1984 | 676,204 | 2.42% | 553,397 |
| 1985 | 689,507 | 1.97% | 569,538 |
| 1986 | 704,515 | 2.18% | 586,151 |
| 1987 | 715,260 | 1.53% | 603,248 |
| 1988 | 727,561 | 1.72% | 620,843 |
| 1989 | 743,023 | 2.13% | 638,952 |
| 1990 | 760,148 | 2.30% | 657,589 |
| 1991 | 776,848 | 2.20% | 676,770 |
| 1992 | 793,594 | 2.16% | 696,510 |
| 1993 | 807,601 | 1.77% | 716,826 |
| 1994 | 822,150 | 1.80% | 737,734 |
| 1995 | 838,898 | 2.04% | 759,253 |
| 1996 | 858,364 | 2.32% | 781,399 |
| 1997 | 875,811 | 2.03% | 804,191 |
| 1998 | 891,176 | 1.75% | 827,648 |
| 1999 | 914,106 | 2.57% | 851,789 |
| 2000 | 933,935 | 2.17% | 876,634 |
| 2001 | 955,076 | 2.26% | 902,204 |
| 2002 | 974,271 | 2.01% | 928,519 |
| 2003 | 992,046 | 1.82% | 955,602 |
| 2004 | 1,006,317 | 1.44% | 983,476 |
| 2005 | 1,024,035 | 1.76% | 1,012,162 |
| 2006 | 1,041,685 | 1.72% | 1,041,685 |

# Appendix C

## Worldwide Growth Since 1901

The growth data for the entire General Conference is better than that of North America. This includes divisions where pastors are settled and those which are not. The average annual growth rate for the entire church from 1901 to 2006 is 5.1229774%.

| Year | Membership | Growth Rate | Average Growth rate |
|------|-----------|-------------|---------------------|
| 1901 | 78,188 | 3.2% | 79,649 |
| 1902 | 73,522 | 6.0% | 83,729 |
| 1903 | 77,554 | 5.5% | 88,018 |
| 1904 | 81,721 | 5.4% | 92,527 |
| 1905 | 87,311 | 6.8% | 97,268 |
| 1906 | 91,531 | 4.8% | 102,251 |
| 1907 | 94,048 | 2.7% | 107,489 |
| 1908 | 97,579 | 3.8% | 112,996 |
| 1909 | 100,931 | 3.4% | 118,784 |
| 1910 | 104,526 | 3.6% | 124,870 |
| 1911 | 108,975 | 4.3% | 131,267 |
| 1912 | 114,206 | 4.8% | 137,991 |
| 1913 | 122,386 | 7.2% | 145,061 |
| 1914 | 125,844 | 2.8% | 152,492 |
| 1915 | 136,879 | 8.8% | 160,304 |
| 1916 | 141,488 | 3.4% | 168,517 |
| 1917 | 153,857 | 8.7% | 177,150 |
| 1918 | 162,667 | 5.7% | 186,225 |
| 1919 | 178,239 | 9.6% | 195,765 |

| 1920 | 185,450 | 4.0% | 205,794 |
| 1921 | 198,088 | 6.8% | 216,337 |
| 1922 | 208,771 | 5.4% | 227,420 |
| 1923 | 221,874 | 6.3% | 239,071 |
| 1924 | 238,657 | 7.6% | 251,318 |
| 1925 | 250,988 | 5.2% | 264,193 |
| 1926 | 261,834 | 4.3% | 277,728 |
| 1927 | 274,064 | 4.7% | 291,956 |
| 1928 | 285,293 | 4.1% | 306,912 |
| 1929 | 299,555 | 5.0% | 322,635 |
| 1930 | 314,253 | 4.9% | 339,164 |
| 1931 | 336,046 | 6.9% | 356,539 |
| 1932 | 362,101 | 7.8% | 374,805 |
| 1933 | 384,151 | 6.1% | 394,006 |
| 1934 | 404,509 | 5.3% | 414,191 |
| 1935 | 422,968 | 4.6% | 435,410 |
| 1936 | 438,139 | 3.6% | 457,715 |
| 1937 | 452,758 | 3.3% | 481,164 |
| 1938 | 469,951 | 3.8% | 505,814 |
| 1939 | 486,670 | 3.6% | 531,727 |
| 1940 | 504,752 | 3.7% | 558,967 |
| 1941 | 520,644 | 3.1% | 587,603 |
| 1942 | 535,134 | 2.8% | 617,706 |
| 1943 | 544,710 | 1.8% | 649,350 |
| 1944 | 557,768 | 2.4% | 682,617 |
| 1945 | 576,378 | 3.3% | 717,587 |
| 1946 | 598,683 | 3.9% | 754,349 |
| 1947 | 628,594 | 5.0% | 792,994 |
| 1948 | 672,658 | 7.0% | 833,619 |
| 1949 | 716,538 | 6.5% | 876,325 |
| 1950 | 756,812 | 5.6% | 921,219 |
| 1951 | 803,720 | 6.2% | 968,413 |
| 1952 | 856,463 | 6.6% | 1,018,024 |
| 1953 | 924,822 | 8.0% | 1,070,177 |
| 1954 | 972,071 | 5.1% | 1,125,002 |
| 1955 | 1,006,218 | 3.5% | 1,182,636 |
| 1956 | 1,051,452 | 4.5% | 1,243,222 |
| 1957 | 1,102,910 | 4.9% | 1,306,912 |
| 1958 | 1,149,256 | 4.2% | 1,373,865 |

| | | | |
|---|---|---|---|
| 1959 | 1,194,070 | 3.9% | 1,444,247 |
| 1960 | 1,245,125 | 4.3% | 1,518,236 |
| 1961 | 1,307,892 | 5.0% | 1,596,015 |
| 1962 | 1,362,775 | 4.2% | 1,677,778 |
| 1963 | 1,428,352 | 4.8% | 1,763,731 |
| 1964 | 1,508,056 | 5.6% | 1,854,086 |
| 1965 | 1,578,504 | 4.7% | 1,949,070 |
| 1966 | 1,661,657 | 5.3% | 2,048,921 |
| 1967 | 1,747,614 | 5.2% | 2,153,887 |
| 1968 | 1,845,183 | 5.6% | 2,264,230 |
| 1969 | 1,953,078 | 5.8% | 2,380,226 |
| 1970 | 2,051,864 | 5.1% | 2,502,164 |
| 1971 | 2,145,061 | 4.5% | 2,630,349 |
| 1972 | 2,261,403 | 5.4% | 2,765,102 |
| 1973 | 2,390,124 | 5.7% | 2,906,757 |
| 1974 | 2,521,429 | 5.5% | 3,055,670 |
| 1975 | 2,666,484 | 5.8% | 3,212,211 |
| 1976 | 2,810,606 | 5.4% | 3,376,772 |
| 1977 | 2,949,758 | 5.0% | 3,549,763 |
| 1978 | 3,117,535 | 5.7% | 3,731,617 |
| 1979 | 3,308,191 | 6.1% | 3,922,787 |
| 1980 | 3,480,518 | 5.2% | 4,123,750 |
| 1981 | 3,668,087 | 5.4% | 4,335,009 |
| 1982 | 3,897,814 | 6.3% | 4,557,090 |
| 1983 | 4,140,206 | 6.2% | 4,790,549 |
| 1984 | 4,424,612 | 6.9% | 5,035,968 |
| 1985 | 4,716,859 | 6.6% | 5,293,959 |
| 1986 | 5,092,503 | 8.0% | 5,565,168 |
| 1987 | 5,445,249 | 6.9% | 5,850,270 |
| 1988 | 5,816,767 | 6.8% | 6,149,978 |
| 1989 | 6,260,617 | 7.6% | 6,465,040 |
| 1990 | 6,694,880 | 6.9% | 6,796,242 |
| 1991 | 7,102,976 | 6.1% | 7,144,412 |
| 1992 | 7,498,653 | 5.6% | 7,510,419 |
| 1993 | 7,962,210 | 6.2% | 7,895,176 |
| 1994 | 8,382,558 | 5.3% | 8,299,644 |
| 1995 | 8,812,555 | 5.1% | 8,724,833 |
| 1996 | 9,296,127 | 5.5% | 9,171,804 |
| 1997 | 9,702,834 | 4.4% | 9,641,674 |

| | | | |
|---|---|---|---|
| 1998 | 10,163,414 | 4.7% | 10,135,614 |
| 1999 | 10,939,182 | 7.6% | 10,654,860 |
| 2000 | 11,687,239 | 6.8% | 11,200,706 |
| 2001 | 12,320,844 | 5.4% | 11,774,515 |
| 2002 | 12,894,015 | 4.7% | 12,377,721 |
| 2003 | 13,406,554 | 4.0% | 13,011,829 |
| 2004 | 13,936,932 | 4.0% | 13,678,422 |
| 2005 | 14,399,072 | 3.3% | 14,379,164 |
| 2006 | 15,115,806 | 5.0% | 15,115,806 |

www.ingramcontent.com/pod-product-compliance
Lightning Source LLC
Chambersburg PA
CBHW061153040426
42445CB00013B/1665